This book belongs to

_____

This book is dedicated to my children - Mikey, Kobe, and Jojo.

Copyright © 2023 Grow Grit Press LLC. All rights reserved. No part of this book may be reproduced in any form without permission in writing from the publisher. Please send bulk order requests to info@ninjalifehacks.tv

Paperback ISBN: 978-1-63731-810-2
Hardcover ISBN: 978-1-63731-812-6
eBook ISBN: 978-1-63731-811-9
Board Book ISBN: 978-1-63731-813-3

Printed and bound in the USA.
NinjaLifeHacks.tv

Ninja Life Hacks®
by Mary Nhin

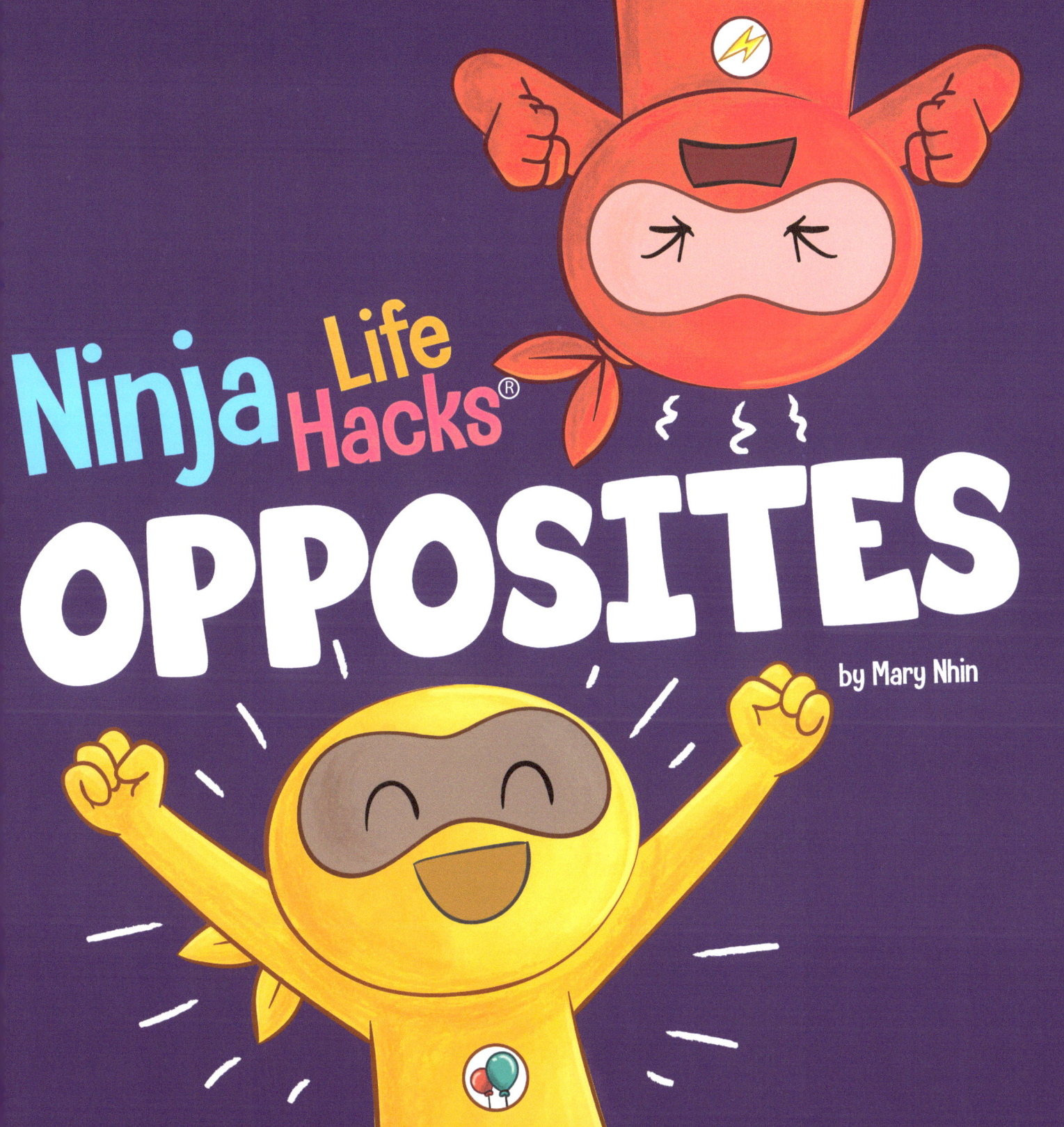

Ninjas know their opposites,
Like what is **up** or **down**.

When you're **positive**, you smile,
But when you're **mad**, you frown.

Careful! Red means **stop**.
OK, now the light's green – **GO**!

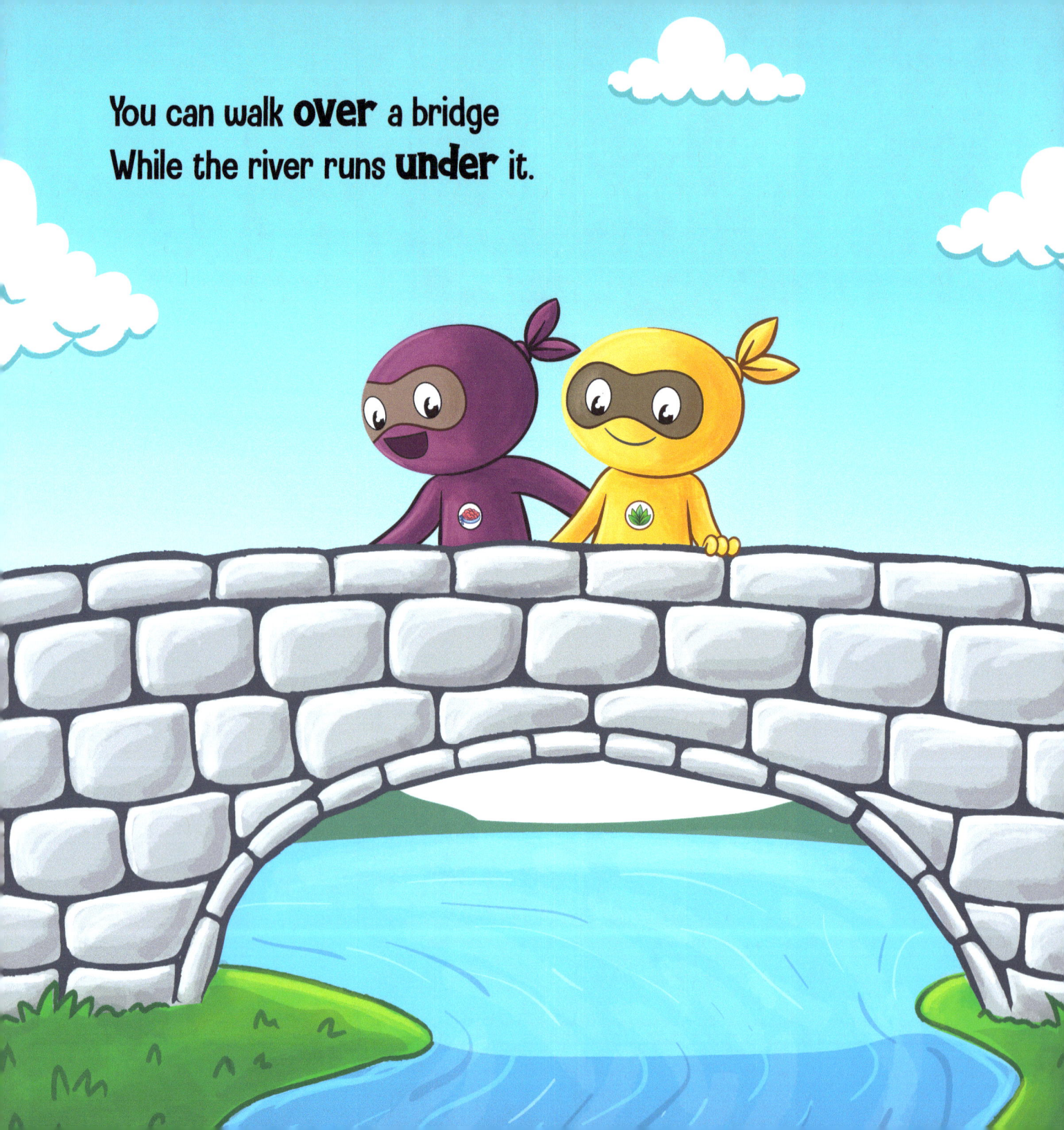
You can walk **over** a bridge
While the river runs **under** it.

At a football game, it's OK to be **loud**,
But in a library, you must be **quiet**.

Cocoa is steaming **hot**,
While chocolate milk is **cold**.

A baby is very **young**,
While grandparents are usually **old**.

That direction is **left**,
While this direction is **right**.

When you're out of the house, you're **outside**,
But in your bedroom, you're **inside**.

When you spill juice, the table is **wet**,
But once you clean it, it will be **dry**.

When you crouch on the floor, you're **low**,
But standing on a chair, you're very **high**!

When rain cancels your plans, you're **disappointed**,
But when the weather is nice, you're **glad**.

Now you know **many** opposites,
Before you may have only known a **few**,

And since ninjas know their **opposites**,
You may be a ninja too!

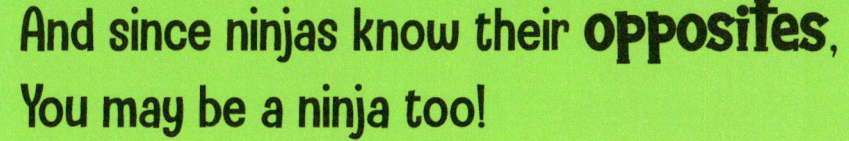

Continue the learning with our fun lesson plans which include superpower skills practice, STEM activity, craft, and more! Visit ninjalifehacks.tv

 @marynhin @officialninjalifehacks
#NinjaLifeHacks

 Ninja Life Hacks

Mary Nhin   Ninja Life Hacks

@officialninjalifehacks

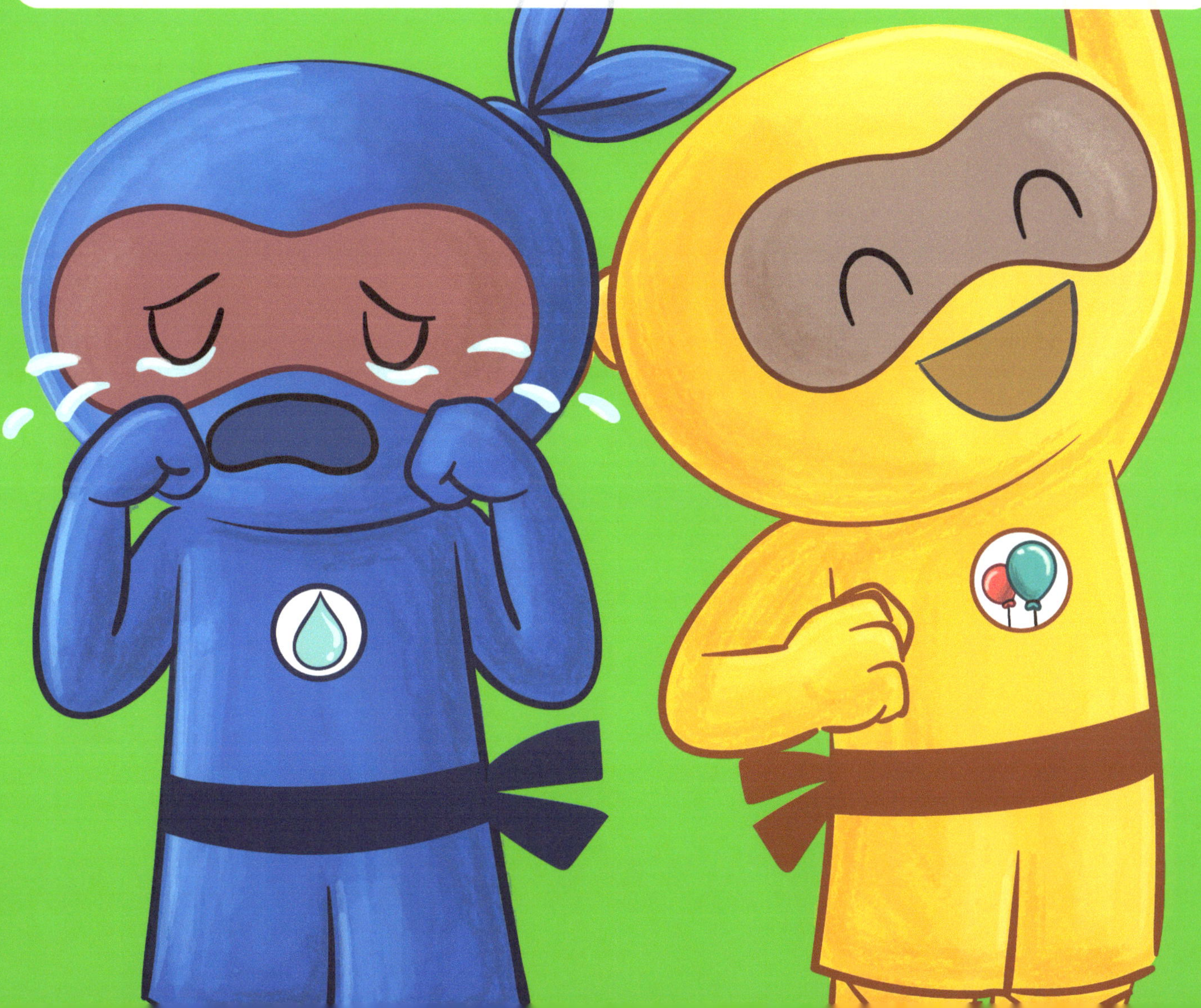

www.ingramcontent.com/pod-product-compliance
Lightning Source LLC
Chambersburg PA
CBHW041526070526
44585CB00002B/101